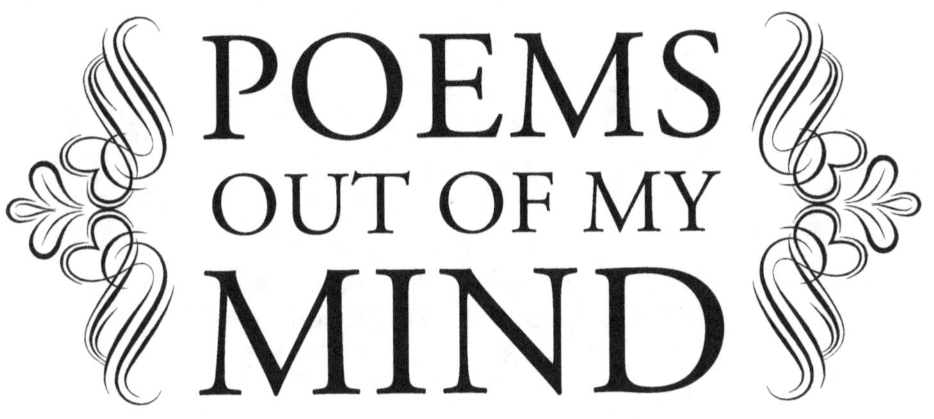

POEMS
OUT OF MY
MIND

KATHLEEN A. DUBÉ

ISBN 979-8-88851-022-3 (Paperback)
ISBN 979-8-88851-024-7 (Hardcover)
ISBN 979-8-88851-023-0 (Digital)

Covenant Books
11661 Hwy 707
Murrells Inlet, SC 29576
www.covenantbooks.com

This book is dedicated to my loving family, all those who came into and enriched my life and especially, my daughter, Janet, without whom this poetry book would not have been possible.

Love to All

CONTENTS

LIFE

We come into this world

With body and soul

And we leave

With less.

OUR PROMISES

It's for each and every one of us,

To thank God for our good fortune,

Appreciate God's beauty in Nature,

Find solace in God in our sorrow,

Pray for courage when needed,

And to love, forgive, and,

Help each other for all of our lives.

TROUBLES

Troubles galore.
What's one to do?
Sort them out one by one.
That's the clue.

THE DIVINE WHO

Who decided the sky would be blue,
And the grass and trees the color green?
Who decided all this,
For me and you?
Who decided flowers would come in many colors,
Such a splendid work of art,
Ever so pleasing to the eye,
And especially to all lovers.
The birds that don't fall,
And airplanes too,
They all somehow stay up there,
Oh, the wonder of it all!
Who can explain this world to us,
Plants and animals and people too,
We all inhabit this land we're on,
Was it all put together without much fuss?
Who decided the world would go on,
Be fruitful and multiply,
The WORD was made,
As each newborn babe was born.
What it is, is naught but mystery,
As we go about our busy lives,
Not knowing it all but continuing our good works,
And leaving the questions to history.

A Birthday Wish

Tick, tock, tick, tock,
On and on goes the clock,
Still trying to live each day,
With some promises and hope.

Knock, knock on the door goes Father Time,
Not on his, but on mine,
Birthday time is here again,
Without fail, each season, every year.

Yes, another year older,
Maybe another year bolder,
But how about wiser,
For that is what I'd choose?

So, I wish Happy Birthday with glee,
To others who share today with me,
I know it's a blessing to be alive,
To experience the very mysteries of life.

Children of the Universe

Free or lost,
Does she know, does anyone?
Dancing in the moonlight,
A free spirit or lost child?
Does she even belong to the universe,
Wandering, wandering, wandering?

All who meet her cannot but love,
This odd and forsaken one,
With moondust in her eyes,
Afraid to turn around,
To see behind her what haunts her so.

Run, run, barefoot, who needs shoes?
But there's nowhere to go and nowhere to hide,
Though one may travel to the ends of the Earth,
To seek and to find,
We must realize that we are all of but one soul,
And we are all children of the universe.

Our World

Yes, it's a beautiful world,
Look at the beautiful mountains,
All the calming scenic lakes, great oceans too,
And the many breathtaking waterfall fountains.

Each country lands so diverse,
Each with their own customs and traditions,
Their coverings, foods, all so very different,
Their landmasses are all calculated positions.

God, our Creator,
Did His very best,
With the sunsets and different seasons,
No, we cannot put Him to any test.

None can compare, and those who deny,
The very existence of a Super Power,
Creating the very moment of a beautiful birth,
Even as we visualize the most exquisite, rare flower.

Mountains

We can climb or tunnel through,
But we can't move them,
However, there is a Higher Power like none,
Stronger than a diamond gem.

So we must acknowledge,
Our limitations,
Carry on at our best,
And deal with our tribulations.

Blessed and fortunate to be given special gifts,
To do all great things,
And though peoples are not alike,
We all benefit what talent brings.

Life is a game of chance,
Good luck whenever to behold,
Much can be accomplished,
For those who are so bold.

Robin, Robin Redbreast

So classy, yet conservative,
In your vest of red,
A brown color for your coat,
Strutting on the ground, a look or two ahead.
There are others more beautiful than you,
But you capture my attention,
Diligently searching,
Although not deer, your own venison.
You come and go,
Home will be wherever you feel free,
Perhaps, after my view,
Time to move on silently.
Everything is but temporary,
We can only hold joy for so long,
Goodbye for now,
For I don't know where you really belong.

Sorrows

For each sorrowing time we suffer a loss in life,
We can become closer to our Heavenly Father in our strife,
To those who seek, He dispenses courage, faith, and such,
And of His love, we can never have too much.

Though the load is heavy as you mourn your loss,
You are, in fact, taking your turn carrying the Cross,
May His bountiful love in your heart bestow,
A relief of that sorrow and the letting of
        peace and tranquility to flow.

WORDS OF COMFORT

What words of comfort can you say to him?
Nothing much, because there's a place we've not been,
They must suffer alone and this burden bear,
Tho' their loved ones' hearts break and tear.

They go through stages, they say, of anger and acceptance,
And their life passes by full of repentance,
But their courage is remarkable, as they answer God's call,
Full of faith and trust, all those great and small.

We try to pity, but of that they will have none,
As they prepare for life's last journey, a walk into the rising sun,
And when my time comes, Lord, will you bear with me,
If I do not measure up to those already gone to Thee?

For Uncle Paul, Aunt Irene, and family

DECISIONS, DECISIONS, DECISIONS

Will everybody always,
Be able to agree?
Guess not,
A lot of decisions need to be made, you see.

Big ones, small ones,
What should I wear today?
Do I need to see a doctor?
Should I wait to buy this on payday?

Who is my friend?
Who is not?
Should I keep this relationship,
In this mystery I am caught.

Decisions, decisions,
We all have free will,
So everybody agreeing to everything,
Is just not possible, only goes uphill.

Books or Lists

There are two things in life,
That will drive you to distinction,
No, we're not failing ourselves,
And we're not depending on intuition.

It's just the way it is,
It's all part of life,
And we have to comprehend,
Carry on with the extra strife.

And what are these two things?
Oh yes, waiting and forgetting,
So what to do?
A book or list is what you need getting.

A book is very handy,
While waiting in a doctor's office,
Or held up in long traffic,
So good for us to practice.

Now, a list can also be very handy,
Forgetting, I believe,
They say only gets worse with age,
Or am I being deceived?

I sigh as maybe do you,
But together we'll conquer the world,
Keep our minds and bodies together,
With some very helpful glue!

THE BIBLE

The Bible, open book to all,

No owner can claim it,

Many years ago written,

Not meant to edit.

The Testaments,

Old, followed by the New,

Authors, Matthew, Mark, Luke, and John,

To name a few.

Enrich one's faith,

Open the Bible at your leisure,

Blessings abound to readers,

None other book can measure.

Forgiveness

Not so easy to do,
A lot of blame,
Can go around,
And that is mighty shame.

Begin with self,
The hardest of all,
We all make mistakes,
That is the call.

And when it comes to others,
Go the extra mile,
You can choose to do it,
Because inside you will free that smile.

If for some reason,
An apology answer is needed,
And yet still none received,
Forgiveness from afar is heeded.

Nonrhyming

Win battles or the war,
Which to choose?
Win the battle,
Or the war?
Arguments can be stressful and unnerving,
Really get you nowhere,
So go with the chosen battle,
A lot of wasted energy to win a war,
Do so compromise,
Or choose to agree or disagree!

THE CATERPILLAR

Oh, their big wide eyes,
Such wonder!
The fuzzy brown caterpillar,
Captures their childish attention.

There's no rhyme or reason,
Just simplicity,
In the purest form,
That magical time of childhood.

It doesn't bite,
It tickles says she,
Look how it makes itself into a ball,
She's sure it will turn into a butterfly.

Only five years old,
Nadine and Colette,
The backyard is a wonderful place,
With all kinds of creatures and a very short time to play.

SEQUINED GIRL

Sequined girl, sequined girl,
Oh, how she loves to sparkle,
Oh, how she loves to shine,
Can she really be all mine,
And when I see those sequins on the ground,
I know that she's been around.

Oh, sequined girl, you have my heart,
Always did right from the start,
She's so fancy, she's so free,
All I want is that girl for me.

Settle down with me, oh my love,
And we'll have such happiness from above,
We won't always be so young and carefree,
Time erodes all that lives, you see,
So let me take good care of you,
And our love will always shine and sparkle too.

Written as a song by inspiration from my daughter, Janet

AMBER

Tiny little Princess,
Gone to yonder above,
Answering to Heaven's call,
Leaving the family you so love.

Though all are grieving your loss,
You brought such comfort and joy,
So special were you,
They wouldn't have traded you for the most expensive toy.

You leave other furry friends,
One more special to you than the others,
And though you were first,
You accepted a sister and brothers.

You will be remembered always,
In everyone's hearts so true,
Tiny, but ever so feisty,
Where that came from, there's no clue.

Good night, our sweet little one,
Gone from a loving home,
Be at peace forever,
No longer a need to roam.

Love, from your family

MAINE

Blessed with an ocean side,
One of fifty,
A vacation land to many,
A homeland to the thrifty,
Way up there, the right-hand corner,
Of our country, true,
How it stayed so beloved,
It's a personal choice, others not a clue,
Some moved to the big cities,
Restless, a change of action,
Desirous of fame or fortune,
New careers also a faction,
Still, there are those,
Heading opposite in that direction,
Drawn by the ocean's breeze,
For years, a very long vacation.

My Beautiful Wife
(A Memoir From Rick to Doreen)

An angel from above,
Has left me brokenhearted,
She was my one and only true love,
My beautiful wife.

Way too soon,
And way too young,
She was my world, my stars, my moon,
My beautiful wife.

Though gone, not a minute forgotten,
And my heart still aches,
For the moment I met her, I was besotten,
My beautiful wife.

There is no reasoning or answer as to why,
Sometimes, we're just left in the dark,
For I don't know why you had to die,
My beautiful wife.

Together we will be,
But the time must be right,
A wise One knows all,
Life's plans for you and others and me.

THE BUTTERFLY

If something else I could be,
I would choose to be a butterfly so beautiful and free,
Nestled in my snug cocoon,
My arrival timed to be very soon.

Then everyone would stand in awe,
In amazement like nothing else they ever saw,
Free to go wherever I choose,
With time and space, never a worry to lose.

Such a carefree way of life,
Spreading my beauty with no concerns or strife,
And if I should be passing by,
Please don't catch me - just say hi!

Our Saving Grace

When upon the turbulent waters,
We are tossed,
You are our Saving Grace,
And we no longer are lost.

You are,
Our crowning glory,
The beloved Son of the Father,
Sent to fulfill the Nativity Story.

Life's many storms,
And its glooms at best,
Shall not falter us,
As we wait to be Your table guest.

Life need not be,
Such an unsurmountable test,
You gave us hope and forgiveness,
Until we meet at our final rest.

In the darkness,
We are not captive,
You are the Light of the World,
Who came to teach us the Truth and the
        Way and how we should live.

HAPPINESS

Spread a little happiness or cheer,
Whether a good deed,
Or if you can, an extra dollar bill,
It doesn't hurt, if you will.

Life can be difficult to many,
All kinds of issues exist,
A thank-you is always good,
And you know you should.

What comes around goes around,
Life is too short,
We only have so much time,
And especially when I have to rhyme!

Conscience and Common Sense

Are they,
The same thing?
Not really,
But they do sort of belong to the same ring.

I guess they're like cousins,
A little more distant group,
Because although they belong in the same family,
In the kettle, there's all kind of soup.

Conscience is more spiritual,
And what about common sense?
Character? Inbred? DNA?
An answer please, before I turn to yoga and the incense.

Both are very good,
So very important to know,
And they both will carry us on,
In life, so that we will grow.

The World

The world is a stage,
Evr'y country looking out its window,
Waiting for the next crisis or political act,
And that's a fact.

The world holds its breath,
What will come next?
Turmoil in a faraway country,
USA blesses its bounty.

Involvement in world affairs,
Cannot be avoided,
We all live on the same Earth,
Since the beginning of man's birth.

So get together, all you countries,
Be it friend or foe,
Blend together all your troubles galore,
And maybe tomorrow wars will be no more.

A Soldier

He/she was a soldier going into battle,
So brave and true with a question of no return,
Earnest in facing death like a cobra's rattle,
And a lesson in fate to learn.
They face WAR, the biggest battle of a night,
And as yet, there is no cure,
Yes, they fought with all their might,
How much could they endure?
Their courage is remarkable, not so like me,
"But I do not remember it," one said,
They did all this so that we would all be free,
As one lay there and bled.
Now they go on as one must do,
You must not forever stay down,
There is so much waiting ahead for you,
In your tears and sorrows you must not drown.
Look ahead, soldier, to the future,
It can be as clear as a bell,
Much mending is to be done with a fine suture,
And a far way to go - as this story will tell.

Too Young to Die

Soldier boy, soldier girl, you've answered the call,
To serve in the MILITARY,
The brave, one and all.
Though on 9-11 our country faced mortal strife,
Would war accomplish a nation's goal,
Or waste another life?
For some are only in their 20s, even 19 or 18 years of age,
Fulfilling their honorable duty,
Leaving their mark on history's page.
So, soldier boy, soldier girl, we grieve all your losses,
And unite in prayer,
As they set up more rows of crosses.
Know that through our tears you stand mighty tall,
While we urge all our leaders to be sure, so very sure,
Because they're too young to die, these heroes all.

Peace
Be a Foe or Friend

What a haughty word,
Because it will take some doing,
Doesn't come with a list of directions,
Won't downright tolerate any booing.

What a haughty word,
Taking it with a grain of salt,
Just won't work today,
And you will be called on fault.

What a haughty word,
You won't get away with much,
Peace makes you take a stand,
Even when we don't really want to touch.

What a haughty word,
It forces us to examine our deepest thoughts,
And to think wearily of the bloodshed,
In all the wars we've fought.

What a haughty word,
Because we won't be able to ignore,
The open handshake,
That we refused before.

What a haughty word,
Because PEACE demands an answer,
Or we will pay the ultimate price,
And continue on with the cancer.

What a haughty word,
It allows everyone to be a friend,
By changing the way some people think,
And bringing PEACE to ALL in the very end.

9/11/2001

Everyone gasped,
Mother, father, sister, brother,
We cannot believe our eyes,
Hands to mouth a cry to smother.

Helpless we stared,
The atrocities we were witness to,
All those poor trapped souls,
What could we do?

And those in the streets running to cover,
It's an insane scene at best,
All covered with the falling ash,
Trying to find a safety nest.

The towers falling with pancake effect,
It was truly beyond amazement,
And for so many no escaping,
As some fell to the pavement.

Yes, we remember,
No, we will never forget,
How evil took command,
In the form of a jet.

Yet, America courageously survived,
We stayed strong and held on to the courage test,
Rebuilding with sweat, tears, heart, and faith,
And today "Ground Zero" land is rainbow blest.

9/11 "Let's Roll"

When things go so very wrong,
As they sometimes do,
And the days seem so very long,
After that tragedy we quite knew.

Oh, that tragic 9-11 day we'll always remember,
Heroes on every level,
Yes, we remember as our hearts did break,
And the memories of the brave we'll always revel.

Sadly, year after year the remembrance is still great,
How could we ever forget?
Never, we say, because of that sorrowing fate,
For it's in their honor that we beget.

Time heals all wounds, they say,
But not so easily done with this,
For it was far too magnanimous,
And now all we can do for those all lost is send
        above a prayer and a loving kiss.

THE SURVIVOR TREE

A pear tree,
Not an apple one,
Rescued and brought back to new life,
Might God's will be done.

Never again a repeat,
Of Adam and Eve's original sin,
Who disobeyed His Word,
Denying us a world that should have been.

The Memorial's water baptizing new souls,
Cascading the walls, rippling down,
Lovingly watched over by,
The Survivor Tree that was found.

It was nurtured year after year,
Knowing it must survive,
To give us hope,
And after many long years again alive.

Along with the names,
Of all those loved ones we lost,
And 9-11 destruction now a thing of the past,
A new World Trade Center is back in spite of the horrific cost.

So we should mourn no more,
We have at last found solace and peace,
Ground Zero land no longer exists,
As our tears dry up and evermore cease.

Today the Survivor Tree lives on,
As so do we,
It's also what our loved ones would want,
And now we too can give our thanks to that special pear tree.

This poem is about a special pear tree that was saved after being almost completely destroyed after the 9/11 tragedy in New York City. It survived after being nurtured and lovingly taken care of for a number of years and was finally brought back home to the 9/11 Memorial at the new World Trade Center in New York City.

Know Thy Faith
(On the Fifth Anniversary of 9/11)

For sure, there is still the pain of 9-11,
But not without hope,
Yes, the knees get weak again,
The stomach sick and the tears still sting,
So what do we have left?
It's all beyond my scope,
And I need to hold on to something,
Well, so don't you?
I know I have my thoughts,
And I know I have free will,
To do whatever.
But what I think what God,
Really wants us to know,
Especially in times of suffering,
Is His simple yet powerful request,
Know thy faith!

THE ONLY FRIEND

Tormented soul, what have you done?
Oh, what battles have you won?
What wealth have you gained,
When all your loved ones you have maimed?
For you alone created this mess,
Got caught up in some destructive web, I guess.
Sought by a deadly spider, cunning and swift,
From only so far you can drift.
Creating more havoc than you'll ever know,
And a hell waiting below.
Time is not on your side,
This progressive illness your groom or bride.
Death and destruction are the name of the game,
We pity you not, just the same.
For the choice is yours,
Only you can open those locked doors.
Remember, just as you reap what you sow,
God help your little ones when they grow.
And when all is said and done,
Your accomplishments amount to none.
Can't you see the dangers ahead,
An obituary about you that's just been read?
For the bottle's your only "Friend,"
In the end.

GOD BLESS YOU

God bless you in your losses.
God bless you in your sufferings.
God bless you in the loss of your dreams.
God bless you in your troubles and tribulations.
God bless you when you are hurting.
God bless you in your daily stressors and struggles.
God bless you when you are ignored or helpless.
And God bless you

whenever you are in need.

A Tribute to Vietnam Veterans

On the battlefield, the brave young soldier faces a hell on earth,
He returns broken in spirit and a man much older.

It was not of his choice - the countries decide,
They are not allowed to give their voice.

So one must do what one must do, and they can only do their best,
Those brave young men marching away, two by two.

It was a war, a controversial one with high ideals at the start,
To save humanity, for aggression had begun.

He follows his orders, and then off he goes to the
        battlefield, a place of hell on earth,
The brave young soldier, unaware of the reality of his woes.

But faces it he does to die or live, all of
        his heart and mind and soul,
He puts on the line to give.

It's an ungodly task, this right to kill.
How dare we strike that blow!
Yet they must force themselves, sick in gut, their drill.

No man, woman, or child is safe in that hell on earth.
The innocents will suffer too.
It seems all human beings have lost their worth.

It's so very senseless, but we acknowledge this is war,
And war is a living hell, we know, though
        we try to keep a vision afar.

That someday peace will reign supreme - this
        is the goal that we will strive for,
Oh yes, this surely our dream.

We hear that Vietnam was such a place, and
        the best again were called to fight,
As one race fought another race.

It was inhumanity for some time to come, this war in Vietnam,
A war that no one was destined to have won.

It went on and on, no end was in sight,
Morale was quite low and almost gone.

But the day came when some sense was made,
And the brave soldier was called home, but alas, to no fame.

He held his head up high, but upon his face, the people spat,
Did they not understand his sigh?

For it was not of his own choosing, he did
        but his country's ordered duty,
His very own precious freedom losing.

As he went into that war of hell and did the
        very best a soldier could do,
And later wait for others, their story to tell.

DON'T WORRY

Don't worry,
Because it won't get you a day longer,
Doesn't stop a fatal illness,
Only faith can make you stronger.

Don't worry,
Sad to say,
But you can get a grip,
For grief is here to stay.

Don't worry,
The rich get richer,
And the poor get poorer,
Just get in the game and be the pitcher.

Don't worry,
Business breaks come and go,
Here today, gone tomorrow,
And loss can be such a devastating blow.

Don't worry,
Life goes along, don't try to thwart,
But guess what,
I'm the world's worst worrywart.

LIES

Ooh, ooh, ooh,
That is one touchy subject,
What do we do with it,
Not something we can, not an object?

Is it useful?
Can be to some?
Well, it depends,
Can it be used in fun?

We get into some gray area here,
We know it's ingrained in society,
Find it all over the place,
Well, let's not forget about piety.

It also can get serious, complicated,
Needs a lot of careful thought,
Better to beware,
Wish it were just something simple in a
    store that we could have bought.

I Fell Out of Bed This Morning

Yes, I fell out of bed this morning,
You guessed it,
Friday the 13th,
Thank goodness, didn't hurt a bit.

Lovely way to start the morning,
It's happened before,
Don't I ever learn,
Before I start walking into a door.

Everything happens for a reason,
Are you kidding me?
Just keep on picking yourself up,
And go on with a life so free.

DOWNLOAD

There's just too much stuff,
Going on,
In the world.

All kinds of emotions,
Flying around,
And all about being hurled.

Words carelessly tossed about,
Tensions beyond imagination,
Inappropriate anger.

Some calmness,
Should be in order,
Not left in a closet on a hanger.

Looking down,
Disappointment galore,
God surely didn't want this way for us.

The end may not yet be here,
So we should use wisely our time,
And stop all the gore and fuss.

Tears and Feelings

A summer's breeze ever so soothing,
A furrowed brow smoothing.
A cool drink for a parched throat,
A soprano's note.
An April shower so refreshing,
My brother's keeper - a blessing.
A cool hand on warm forehead,
"Why are you worried?" someone said.
A mother's tender hand,
Someone understands.
Welcomed relief from built-up tensions,
"God bless you!" someone mentions.
Renewed strength to go on,
Replenishing a supply almost gone.

THE LADY STANDS TALL

The LADY of metal and stone,
So very mysterious, shrouded in solitude,
Given to us by a country great,
In all her splendor and magnitude.

Her glowing tiara in the night,
Giving calm over tempest storm,
Holding freedom's torch in her untiring outstretched arm,
With ne're a doubt the very best of form.

She welcomes all that come to her shores,
The first loving sight after a long journey,
Giving hope and faith,
To all those multitudes yearning.

Many are grateful for opportunity given,
And share their thanks again,
This special 100th year,
As she ages gracefully to all her friends.

Sometimes a "paint and powder job" are needed true,
But we all know she'll always remain,
Forever in our minds and hearts,
And, we pray, for centuries to come on our terrain.

Life, Liberty, and Justice

It's on all our minds,
But how do we get it all together?
We just can't all agree,
Instead, we're as breezy as a feather.

Protests about this and that,
Always some cause out there,
Anger, confusion,
Do they always have to be somewhere?

Division, division, division,
Our heads are spinning out of control,
Somebody take charge,
And give us a goal.

We can make things better,
Democracy will always rule,
Isn't our country founded on this?
Let's go back to the Golden Rule!

For Levin

LIVING MARTYRS

So, you suffered,
And felt the pain,
Why me, why me,
What's all this in GOD's name?

Were you a chosen one,
To be a living martyr,
To carry on that mission,
For GOD, as a starter?

You and your precious family,
At the very mercy of life,
Striving not as a victim,
But a survivor of that strife.

For the missions will differ,
But all, most surely, will be testing,
And as a chosen one,
Will have from above His greatest blessing.

Inspired by the courage of J.W. and his family in the loss of their son
and all those others who go down a path to carry on with dedicated
missions.

HOMESTEAD SAVIORS

Builders, so dedicated,
All grime and grit,
And the homesteaders,
Helping out too, bit by bit.

Facing unimaginable odds,
With humor, stamina, smarts,
Helping the homesteaders,
With all their hearts.

Whatever cannot be salvaged,
Tearing apart with glee,
Solved most of the problems,
Rebuilding with all their energy.

Modern pioneers,
Daring and brave,
Off-grid life for some,
Family life they so crave.

Whatever's out there,
Does not deter a better life,
Bears, mountain lions, snakes, and wolves,
It's all worth the extra strife.

Marty, the in-charge father,
Matt, the hunter, teachers all,
Misty, the innovative farmer daughter,
Passing on their learned knowledge is their only call.

A Blessed Night

The earth is below a blanket of snow,
The trees in unison sway to and fro,
All tots now sleep in their little white beds,
With dreams of the morrow tucked in their heads.

'Tis now the eve of Christmas night,
And the stars are shining ever so bright,
All signs of life have long since ceased,
For all the world now sleeps in peace.

ANGELS

Look around, see a feather,
It's an angel among us,
Guiding and protecting,
Goodness sakes, stifle that cuss.

They are aware,
Of our needs,
Urging kindness expression,
Not want or greed.

Our best friends,
There to protect,
Always around us,
The pitfalls they detect.

In a chaotic world,
That we live in,
Their presence is strongly needed,
To help us avoid the occasion of sin.

Though, it's a very good thing,
They let us soldier on,
Because we've got the will,
To stay ever strong.

But know that they are there,
In good times or bad,
To give a helping hand,
When we are grieving, lost or sad.

A Winter's Day

On a cold winter's day,
They laid their Mom to rest,
Lived a very full life,
For which she was blessed.

She traveled a lot,
With very light feet,
Was gracious to all,
That she would meet.

Her faith ever so strong,
Country, community, and church served well,
And a lesson she would teach,
Take time the roses to smell.

A sound of bugle taps,
Giving honor to you,
The flag folded smartly,
From those men in navy blue.

Oh, time to let go,
Family she loved so very much,
For a heavenly place awaits her,
And they sadly will miss her loving touch.

So goodbye, dear friend,
This poem is written for you,
God's blessings in His Kingdom are awaiting there,
As surely you've earned your due.

For Marlene

WOODS IN WINTER

Fragile sticks, but living ones,
So delicate, so many by the tons,
Elegant setting by the moon,
A winter's haven soon.

Still life at its best,
Waiting for surprising guests.
Little creatures also belong,
Everything perfect, birds sing a fine winter's song.

Food abound for a treat,
Enough for a winter's feast.
Berries and nuts on the branches,
A midnight rendezvous as a shadow dances.

Eerie and ghostly a scene not far,
From my window, am I the star?
Nature has placed me in the center,
With the world our audience and God our mentor.

Struck by the awesome beauty of it all,
In the stillness of the night, I hear a call.
The woods whispering out my name,
Beckoning me to join them in their nightly winter's game.

A Classmate

She's a tiny one but carries a heavy load,
She's a brave one traveling a lonely road,
She's a loving one, though love has been denied her,
She suffers in His imitation, like yonder days that were.

Strong of Faith she's blest, of that there's no doubt,
For isn't that what the world's all about?
So in God's eyes, how she must sparkle,
Like a dewdrop that's quite remarkable.

There are some who will be first in line,
That wish would surely be mine,
So my classmate, save a place for me,
When the heavens open up for us and that
     someday comes that we'll see.

COINCIDENCES

There are no coincidences,
Just a MASTER PLAN out there,
Working behind our backs,
So stay alert, but have no care.

No need for keeping score,
For it's a strange world we're in,
Just keep holding on,
And keeping faith within.

You can look around the corner,
But it doesn't matter at all,
For there are no coincidences,
Things will happen without our call.

A Mother's Prayer:
Be Born Brave

Be born brave, sweet baby,
Lots await to sap your strength,
Difficult times weakening and devouring just maybe,
Your fate at length.
Grow stronger day by day,
Nourish yourself with faith, love, and hope,
Hardship is here to stay,
Learn well now, little one, the lesson is to cope.
It is the strong that survive,
In a world so bold,
The only promise of life is that you are alive,
As of today, so we are told.
So hold on to your dear life,
And come see what's to be,
Regardless of all the strife,
And be as brave as the struggle of your birth prepared you

To come to me!

KIDS

They are special to us,
These kids in each and every way,
No matter how much we holler,
No matter what else we say.
For it's no joyride,
This raising of kids,
There's a high price you pay,
Considering the other bids.
From morn until night,
You worry and fret,
And there's a long way,
For the stakes yet.
You can shoot to the stars,
Almost reaching Mars,
And then descend to the depths of despair,
Beginning again the shreds to repair.
It's a daily grind,
Of routine and task,
Sacrifice, hard work,
Their cooperation is all I ask.
Thank GOD for aspirin,
For the headaches and more,
The endless bickering,
Rebellion galore.
But through it all,
They're a blessing in disguise,
Say the worldly,
And those wise.

For who knows what tomorrow brings,
Renewed hope,
A new world,
And perhaps better things!

THE VASE

The ugliest thing,
But I treasure it,
Why?
Because it was a gift.
Was given to me one day,
No particular reason,
Nothing was special,
It was no holiday season.
I gave it a second look,
Where will it go?
Has to be someplace special,
That only I will know.
It sits on my shelf,
A glance to it now and then,
It couldn't have cost a lot,
How much did they spend?
It's the thought,
We all know,
And I can't believe,
How it gives me a little glow.
Knowing the loving gesture,
And bringing a smile to my face,
For here is where it belongs,
This very special vase.

ROBYN

She would walk into a room,
Adept at conversation,
Would get your eye,
Capture an audience with attention.

Kind and thoughtful,
A soldier girl up to date,
Once saved her sister,
In a crisis fate.

The future held a plan,
That she would someday meet,
A gallant one,
He couldn't wait to greet.

They met in the Military,
That's one lucky guy,
To grab her hand in flight,
And make her his bride.

Two boys followed, making a lot of noise,
To send Robyn in a twirl,
But hastily recovered,
For a girl.

It's anybody's guess,
Why I write all this,
Just thought the world,
Could share in their bliss.

And one would be beholden,
To catch a sight,
As together fearless,
They go running into the night.

The Tiger and the Lily

The Lily ever so delicate and pure,
Was approached by the Tiger,
Who was strong and brave.
He put on a mean face,
Oh, what a way to behave!
And with all his might,
Intimidate he tried.
A roar or two was his sole delight,
Now the Lily, so fair and slight,
Who had much to teach,
With an eloquent flair.
Well, she spoke ever so soft and gently,
Was that Tiger in for a surprise,
As she informed him of,
The ways of the wise.
He cautiously listened,
And soon was besotten,

Not by chance for sure,
With feelings long forgotten.
Thus, inseparable they did become,
Paired off as you'd expect,
As they united into one,
And evolved into the Tigerlily.

SENTIMENT

Some folks are grossly involved,
Others prefer a clean slate,
There is always a middle ground,
And some of our beloved belongings know no date.

What is trash to one,
Is treasure to another's hand,
Childhood items especially difficult to give up,
So hard for some to understand.

Being grown-up happens gradually,
It's not an overnight accomplishment for sure,
Parting is such sweet sorrow, they say,
But facing reality, we must endure!

For C.M.P.

On Becoming a Woman

My daughter, soon you will become a woman,
A miracle will take place within you.
God's puzzle is about to unfold,
As you struggle to understand.
You have grown before my very eyes,
Though I have not always been aware.
With you always, I will be,
There to guide, whenever you need.
Do not be afraid, my daughter,
Go forward and become that woman,
God meant you to be!

For C.M.P. away at G.S. camp

The Woodcutter

What better way,
To let out stress,
And put the headaches out bay,
Than to become a woodcutter,
Let it all hang out,
Let all the energy melt like butter,
The world can treat you rough,
No doubt about it,
So get those boots on and get tough,
And then you'll see the calmness,
Invade your body,
A feeling of warmness,
And all the stress overcome.

For Scott

A Boy and His Grandfather
Version I

A special relationship, a kind of its own,
Love and understanding are all he's known.
Love and kindness a story do tell,
And if wishes could come true from the wishing well.
I would always want the closeness of him,
He's my grandfather, my friend!
The sharing of good times and a talk or two,
A laugh or a joke, hand in hand together like glue.
Inseparable, comforter of little-boy fears,
Brushing away those very little tears.
Time passes, ever so quick,
A blink of an eye and then he's sick.
A stab in the heart,
I wake up with a start.
Confusion and pain,
The tears fall again.
I work it out to my surprise,
'Cause I'm bigger now in size.
I'll have fond memories and know quite well,
A part of him will be with me always, so this story will tell.

A Boy and His Grandfather
Version II

A special relationship, a kind of its own,
Love and understanding are all he's known.
Love and kindness a story do tell,
And if wishes could come true from the wishing well.
I would always want the closeness of him,
He's my grandfather, my friend!
The sharing of good times and a talk or two,
A laugh or a joke, hand in hand together like glue.
Inseparable, comforter of little-boy fears,
Brushing away those very little tears.
Those many walks we took down "Memory Lane,"
Though the day be sunshine or misty rain.
Can only be a treasure to me,
Lock'd away in a heart that was so happy and carefree.
Yes, fond memories I'll have so good and true,
Because I was blessed to have a GRANDFATHER like you!

Ships Passing in the Night

When two people care,
But can't get along,
What to do,
Sounds like an inevitable Swan Song.

Who must change?
Who must compromise,
In order to keep a relationship going?
That's no surprise!

Personalities do differ,
That we know,
And other circumstances,
Will come in tow.

Relationships need nurturing,
A step back now and then,
It can boggle the mind,
How does this happen and when?

Take those ships passing in the night,
Should they just keep cruising,
Or take a leap of faith?
Only chance plays the part for happiness or bruising.

ODE TO KAITLYN

Upon her finger,
A dragonfly alights,
Not mine,
Only hers.

Her special touch,
But my cry of delight,
Who is,
This special one?

This lover of nature,
So little in height,
Seeker of frogs,
With such aplomb and awe.

Don't talk scary,
'Cause she'll show some fright,
Well, she thinks she's big,
But we know better.

Kaitlyn's all of nine years old,
A blossoming beauty in our sight,
Oh, beware the frown on her face,
Or maybe catch the twinkle in her eye.

THE MYSTERY GIRL

There are parallels,
In her life,
Confusing and sometimes,
Causing a bit of strife.
Oh, this mystery one,
Who also has two names,
And is not one,
To shout out any blames.
You know who you are,
Secretly, you smile,
You've still got a way to go,
Continue to walk that mile.
Has sometimes some turmoil,
That can be solved,
Only takes her,
A bit of resolve.
So there's a message,
For all to hear,
To gather up some courage,
As there's crosses to bear.
Challenges,
Don't make her frown,
Always picks herself up,
They don't, for long, keep her down.
She's not a flash,
In the pan,
Knows when,
To take a stand.

She sparkles,
But not in a flashy way,
Just moves about conservatively,
As she goes about her business all day.
She's impressive,
You'd like to stare,
Likes to look fashionable,
What she chooses to wear.
No nitty-gritty for her,
Not a frivolous one to be,
What you get,
Is what you see.
Oh, those comes and goes,
Her will is formidable,
And those ups and downs,
Her stance is admirable.
Be ye not a friend,
But foe,
You will know,
When to go.
She's her own person,
When her hour is darkest,
And things don't look good,
She will fight her hardest.
Strive for her friendship,
Her loyalty beyond measure,
And you will beget,
Something to always treasure.
Things get better for everyone,
When she's right at the gate,
It's a thought to behold,
She'll fill your plate.
For an ending,
She knows to look,
Around the corner,
For there waits the Golden Book.

Sorry, Kait,
To make this an open book,
But if one wants some inspiration,
At this poem, they will know where to look.

TIGER BOY

A blessing when you came into our lives,
Didn't really expect you,
But maybe you were waiting for us,
Because we were just traveling through.

Heading home from a birthday vacation trip,
We casually turned the car around to stop by,
For that upside-down Kittens sign,
That caught our eye.

Rob, Brenda and Kait and Tiger,
Now all together by fate,
What's meant to be will be,
As we gaze at you in front of the fireplace grate.

The Mistress of the house,
Once scolded you with a frown,
"Tiger - no! We don't eat family,"
As you quickly and gently dropped the tiny turtle down.

There were fun times too, though,
Waiting for Kait to come home from school,
For that soccer ball catching game with her,
But patiently waiting was the rule.

Tiger, you didn't always obey,
The Master of the house,
Rob was too soft and easy for you,
But not so Brenda, she was not a mouse.

Many years of love,
Greeting all our guests at the door,
Affectionate and friendly to one and all,
As you roamed the house and floor.

Who could have thought,
That a cat could bring such joy,
When we brought home that day,
Our little kitten, Tiger-boy.

A Tale of a Love Story

'Twas the beginning of two loves,
Came down from Heaven,
By the mischief and action of two doves,
One love would hold strong and fast.

The other broken,
Not meant to last,
Though one love would outweigh,
Through the years,
There would be a reckoning one day,
To face a bond that was still a reality.

That had not gone away,
In totality,
Just know all, that the one love was still there,
To comfort the loss,
That He - in finality would bear.

A QUIET MAN

Helpful,
But in a disappearing way,
Just goes about his business,
Not much of a talker,
Generally has but little to say.

Gentle and kind,
The man that he is,
Ready to give a helping hand,
A person as such is hard to find.

Long in years,
And patriotic too,
He'll well be remembered,
With no thought of asking for any tears.

Yes, he's a quiet and a religious type,
But kept his thoughts to himself,
Wasn't at all about preaching,
Or giving out any hype.

If only many of us those,
Could exist in this life,
With the qualities of him,
A lot more could be written in prose.

No accolades are needed,
For this quiet one,
He soldiered on through life's trials and such,
And his faith he always heeded.

And if there was a wrong,
That he witnessed,
He had a need to right it,
With words ever so strong.

But still quiet and thoughtful to the end,
You'd hardly know what he'd be like,
In chaos or a riot,
This good neighbor friend.

So sleep well, Charlie, with thy long-gone beloved wife,
A good citizen,
A good neighbor friend too,
And a well-lived life.

He was like a whisper
In life
Almost but not quite disappearing.

For C.W.

I Swallowed a Fly

There I was,
Laughing and talking,
Didn't know,
That a fly was stalking.

That is, until I swallowed,
Caught that darn fly in my mouth,
Should have swatted it,
And made it go south.

Oh, how I learned my lesson well,
Look around before you speak,
It sure was a hard one to learn,
So made my knees go weak.

Tomorrow, I may recover,
Got lots of things to do,
But heed my dire warning,
Friend, it could happen to you!

Pie in the Sky

What does that mean?
Who said that?
Where did I hear it?
Just can't pull it out of my hat.

Must be something good though,
Pie is good, right?
Suppose we just reach up,
Grasp that something so far out of our sight.

Washing Machines Eat Socks

Where could they possibly go,
Down the drain?
No, that's not so.

But I put a pair in,
Now there's only one,
I just can't win.

Can't figure it out,
I get so mad,
I want to shout.

Give me a break, I say,
Oh, washing machine,
I got lots of laundry today.

Just have to keep on,
Trying to understand,
Till all this dirty laundry is gone.

If I didn't know better,
I'd say this machine is alive,
And I'd write it a nasty letter.

For making my life,
So very difficult,
And giving me a headache with all this strife.

So what's to do,
With this mountain of unmatched socks,
Dear friends, I ask of you?

THE BAG LADY

That's me!
Wherever I go,
You will recognize,
That lady with bag in tow.

What's in it, you ask,
Though curiosity killed the cat,
Going to visit my family,
Also, carrying her hat.

Yes, she's going to visit her family,
And likes to bring them some treasures,
She would say,
Because it gives them pleasures.

They welcome here,
With open arms,
But only the children squeal with delight,
And the parents sadly need some calms.

It's not only when she visits,
They also come to call,
And there waiting furtively in the corner,
Is that formidable bag for one and all.

She means well,
A house can only hold so much clutter,
But who has the heart and soul to tell,
As her beloved family turns to butter.

A Thousand Words

We must use them,
Or that many words could be left,
Or leave
Our hearts bereft.

There are poems out there waiting,
And words can speak action,
Words need not be extraordinary,
Just some inspiration or consolation.

They can come fast or slow,
Our minds are full of them priceless,
It matters not whether they are yours or mine,
They are all certainly valued no less.

THE MILLENNIUM

Today the world comes together,
Sharing and soaring to new heights,
All are celebrating the last and the first,
With joyous new sounds and sights.

Fireworks sparkles, ice sculptures, and Eiffel thrills,
Excitement is all around,
New Yorkers gather at Times Square,
Oh, was it two million that made such a deafening sound?

It's launching of the new,
And out with the old,
The ball drops by computer,
Now, so we are told.

Each land counts down to midnight,
Y2K - don't worry - be bold!
All will be well as we wait out in the cold.

The morrow did come,
Disrupt it was naught,
The world stood sane,
And then all our worry we forgot.

Technology

Did it just zoom in?
Where did it come from?
A powerful magnet,
To many or just some?

Face-to-face communication,
Phone lines all atwitter,
Social media they call it,
A blessing or a pill to swallow bitter.

What's your email?
A constant query,
The salespeople all ask,
Quite so cheery.

Where's the privacy gone?
Where's that homey feeling so lost?
It's like being in a blender,
That we are tossed.

A hand is lost without that thingamajig in it,
Our sole attention focuses,
On those apps and Google information,
It's sheer magic and some hocus-pocus.

Taking away those smartphones and computers,
May result in a craving,
And questionable behavior,
That can compare to a body raving.

Technology, be it a blessing or a curse,
None the less now is here to stay,
Brings our worlds together,
Just don't get any more complicated, I pray.

THE LAUGHING GIRL

Sweet in nature,
A happy personality,
Friendly as a puppy dog,
Helpful much as she can be.

A lovely soul,
You would want to meet,
Put on this Earth,
All to greet.

She will surely make,
This world a better place,
A sunny disposition,
In all this worldly race.

For T.T.

One More Day

Give me one more day, O Lord,
One more day to settle my affairs,
To heal the wounds I've made with my sword.
Before I climb those stairs,
To seek one more day of beauty,
One more day of wonder,
To carry out my last duty.
Do not yet, one more day, put my life asunder,
One more day to make my peace,
One more day to show my love,
Soon enough my life shall cease.
Grant my wish from above,
I hear the call, that is true,
My house will be in order,
And I will bid adieu.
Why must I be such a bother?
Patience with me, Lord,
I am reluctant to let go,
My life I try to hoard.
Till I see one more sunset, one more torn heart to sew,
I didn't realize how much I would lose,
I guess I didn't appreciate my lot,
One more day, if I may choose.
Then everything, I'll drop,
I want everything to be just so,
I guess it can't be that way,
The time and day are yours, I know,
But all I ask for is - one more day.

Also made into a song

A SIMPLE LIFE

Who doesn't want a simple life?
Well, maybe not everyone,
There are different degrees of energy and curiosity,
One or more levels are desired by some.

However, demand does not keep for all,
Taking in point - getting older,
Some stay young in thought and age,
Others move on less bolder.

But keep in mind,
Jesus led a simple life,
Age was not a factor,
He did not look for strife.

His destiny called to Him,
And He walked the walk,
We need ourselves to take heed,
As He slowly moved about doing His sermon talk.

Now, how do we seniors cope,
An eye out for that simple life,
As a lot gets in our way,
Cutting us clean with life's knife?

Health, finances, losses, all move about,
Catching us off guard,
Through the years,
With no regard.

So struggle as we may,
For that simple life in our sight,
We just go on and on and on,
Cherish what we have with all our might.

THE PINNACLE

Reaching the pinnacle,
Is a long, long road,
But never a thought of giving up,
No matter how heavy was the load.
Always there was a cause,
And keeping an eye on that goal,
Because you can be and you can do,
Whatever it takes to get out of that hole.
All it takes is that first step,
Oh, what a long way to go!
But nothing is impossible,
If I believe it ain't so.
There will be sidetracks,
And confusing signs to sort,
They'll be those who would discourage,
And try to keep you from the port.
But you will arrive,
Maybe not always to glory or fame,
However, that pinnacle you will reach,
And make that claim to your name.
It was always meant to be,
A complex plan for sure,
By a POWER greater,
No matter what one had to endure.
Now, that day has finally come,
Look around and say it is so!
We have finally reached the pinnacle,
And can say "Way to Go."

Monday Blues

Monday, Monday,
That first weekday,
Not my favorite,
Surely, not a fun day.

Back to work,
Earning my pay,
Have to pay the bills,
And a place to stay.

Then, Tuesday through Friday,
Work those days week long,
But looking forward again to the weekend,
The fun days where I belong.

Movies, theater, sports, biking, and shopping too,
Kids along, your choice for sure,
Camping and hiking, keeping in mind,
Those Monday blues for a cure!

Now Can Be Forever

Mourn not my death but rather my life,
Be sorry instead for the hurts and strife,
Is it too late to make amends?
Well, why did you wait so long, my friends?

Remember the tear that you could have wiped away,
Remember the smile that you could have
      brought to my face that day?
I need not be supplied with earthly comforts now,
Today, to a much greater power, I bow.

Hear my words, I beg of you,
That morrow need not come, 'tis true,
If you love me now and be kind to me,
Lest that morrow come,
Then too late forever, you shall be…

Pain

I know pain,
And my pain knows me,
It's always lurking about,
Knows where I'll be.

Though I try to escape,
It's futile for sure,
Never too far away,
Always at my door.

I try to be patient,
Giving it some time,
For nothing is forever,
Not this earthly body of mine.

LOVE

Love didn't fail,
It was there,
In a soft whisper or a tender touch,
On a gloomy day,
Or one so fair.

It burrows into the heart,
Creating a nest,
Smoldering at times,
Or shooting up like a flame,
But always at its best.

For it cannot be diminished,
Through trials or error,
And there it is to stay,
As a welcoming guest,
Yesterday and today, now and forever.

People

People can get,
In the way,
Don't do this and that,
That's what they say.

They tell you what to do,
Okay, that's not wise,
Should I listen,
That's what I surmise.

Life is full of surprises,
And though I will stumble,
Fall I may but then get up,
Life's too hard, I grumble.

However, I'll try the unknown,
That path so uncertain,
Don't discourage me so,
Take away that veil and curtain.

But life's too short, I've heard,
And that's for sure,
Things can go terribly wrong,
Promises can go bleak and blur.

So leave us with hope, faith, and a prayer,
Tomorrow is a brand-new day,
Won't let those years pass me by,
People, step aside for us out of the way.

For J.G. and S.W.

The Necessities of Life

Food, Water, Shelter,
What about Love?
Is that not a basic life necessity?
We know it can be to some,
An elusive gift from above,
There are those fortunate enough,
Early in life,
To be gifted as such,
But for those at a loss,
Will search all life long,
Wondering where they belong,
There will be substitutions,
Power, money, and addictions,
Material belongings for replacement,
Though enough will never be enough,
Until we come to the conclusion,
This reality of life,
That Love is truly a necessity of life.

ROAD TO NOWHERE

Where am I going?
Is there anyone out there in the knowing?
Give me a clue, if you please,
I beg of you, do not laugh or tease.
There are so many stops and go,
Gives me a headache and such, you know.
All those zigzags and different paths to take,
For sure my life is at stake.
So either I go nowhere or take that first step,
To get going, get in the knowing, even get hep.
After all, it's all in the game,
And unfortunately, there's no one else to blame.

THE CROSSROADS OF YOUTH

Which freewill road,
Shall I take,
The one filled with temptations or the straight and narrow one?
It's a decision I'll someday have to make
Along life's journey,
For I'm not so terribly big right now,
But I'll have some guidance true,
And then through all life's trials,
I'll do rightly good, I vow.

Loved More, Never Less

You are loved more than you'll ever know,
It's all inside that we store,
Sorry if not all the time we show,
But understand it's no less,
Than any other gift one can give, I guess,
Though not a Horn of Plenty to sift,
It's give-and-take, an even situation,
As we gravitate to our dual emotions,
For it's not at all a mind-numbing equation,
To conquer our differences,
If we have a mind or a notion.

INDEPENDENT WOMEN

A very fine group, they are!
Unafraid and bold, having vision afar,
Involved with life on a full-time basis,
Watch out for these women that are surely going places.

Oh, they'll be some men who'll want to run them out,
They'll have the envy, that's what it's about,
So, women, stand your ground,
And let them not nudge you aground.

You might stumble and fall,
From places mighty feet tall,
And you'll pay high prices,
But a piece of the cake, you'll have your slices.

Oh yes, unfairly these women will pay,
But nothing will stop them from having their say,
They are surely the greatest,
Born also to blaze the trail, these latest.

So move over, the chauvinistic male,
It's a fact of life not meant to fail,
Independent women have their worth,
And can add to the bounty on earth.

All the while, a compliment to you,
Let's stop this tug-of-war, it's long overdue,
Treat us equal persons, if you please,
Of intelligence and talent, not objects of tease.

Together, we'll win the battles of the world,
And all those hardships of life, we'll surely
overrule!

GRANDCHILD

I am awaiting the birth of our grandchild,
Anxiously waiting for the good news,
A tiny little baby, meek and mild,
With feet so small, they'll ne're even fit a pair of shoes.
It will coo and gurgle and suck its thumb,
Depending on us for all its needs,
And probably wonder at our open-mouthed faces so dumb,
Making its worldly entrance, ready to do all deeds.
Such a sweet little bundle of joy,
Letting us know soon enough who's boss!
Oh, what will it be - a girl or a boy?
And like every other child, it won't be long before asking for a horse.
Making a Mommy and Daddy ever so proud,
As they follow your growth each step of the way,
But just wait, soon those little cries will get ever so loud,
And then before you know it - the baby's all grown up someday.
So enjoy your wee one while you can,
There will be good days and bad ones too,
Together, you'll all explore the treasures of man,
And the wondrous world that God has created for you.

A Poem for Monti

Why did you leave me?
I miss you so,
I hope you are at peace,
Please let me know.
We had such good times together,
Now there will be no more,
You are in a better place,
Though my heart is breaking and sore.
If I could have had a choice,
You would still be by my side,
Nevermore to part,
And we'd still be together walking outside.
Life can give you some pain,
Alas, a lot of sorrow -
But the day will someday come,
When I can look for a tomorrow.

Sisters

She is a dear friend for life.

Is a joy through calm and strife.

Secrets we share.

Takes time to care.

Ever understanding.

Ready to comfort in trials demanding … AND

Silent partner when I'm not at my best …

Chosen for me among all the rest.

Diamonds in the Sky

Diamonds in the night sky,
So very exquisite,
Raining down,
Or shooting across on the fly.

Heavenly made,
Giving us a spectacular view,
Always with perfection,
His actions for us to bade.

One needs not to listen,
For silently they express,
No fireworks needed,
And, oh, how they sparkle and glisten.

From the beginning of the world's creation,
Stars were always present,
Though only one of His great works,
A blessed gift to one and all nation.

For H, T, K, and M.M.

HELLOS AND GOODBYES

We all look forward to Hellos,
Not so for Goodbyes,
Hello is a joyful moment,
While a goodbye can bring on cries.

We will meet again,
You say,
But really, who knows,
What is in the next future days.

Goodbyes have a firmer tone,
An ending for sure,
For the future is more uncertain,
And right now quite a blur.

There is always hope on the horizon,
Faith to hold on to,
That that hello will come again,
And prayers are all we can do.

For H.L., T.D., and K.D.

GROWING OLDER

Not fun,
At all,
I remember when,
I was so tall.

Now, I have an ache,
Here and there,
Guess I'll have to just,
Grin and bear.

There must be,
Some consolation,
I may be older but surely wiser,
So let this be the compensation.

TO VELVET WITH LOVE

We will part, my pet,
In the most painful way,
And the sky will shower tears,
On this very sad day.

We had to let you go,
Quality of life was gone,
Cat heaven awaits you now,
For that is where you belong.

Tears will flow freely,
For some time to come,
No pet can ever take your place,
No, not one.

Heartbreak is never easy,
One must take it on the chin,
For there is no easy answer,
There's no way you can win.

Only God understands pain and joy,
It's too complicated for us,
And we just do our best,
Go on a day at a time without fuss.

So goodbye, my sweet,
Take your leave now,
We will remember you always,
And go on with our lives somehow.

SPOOKY WOODS AT FOX HILL

What's there?
Watch out,
Behind that tree,
Don't move,
Don't shout.

Slowly step back,
Something's out there,
Waiting to pounce on you,
Better to beware.

The fog is heavy,
The night is dark,
What do I hear,
Listen carefully, Hark!

Breathe slowly,
And soon you'll be out,
And away from the talk,
Away from whatever it's all about.

All those rumors,
Were heard for years,
About the Fox Hill Spooky Woods,
Voices and visions that capitulated our fears.

Go home and be safe,
Don't try to explore,
Better to leave the unknown,
Don't open a forbidden door.

Boots

Boots the hunter, fine and sleek,
Watch out, little creatures, she's of a breed not meek,
She loves to play, unwilling to hurt,
A house cat we tried in vain to convert,
With this family, she's here to stay,
Never once went astray,
Ours since a kitten,
We almost named her mitten,
But Boots won our hearts, and that's who she is,
She's our protector, she's a whiz,
She has an adorable face,
With us is her place.

I Ain't the Boss

So what do I care if everything is chaos,
I ain't the boss.

So what do I care if the work don't get done,
I ain't the boss, so for me, it's no fun.

So what if everybody is unhappy and cross,
I ain't the boss.

And who cares if we're far behind our schedule,
It's not my problem, that's my rule.

It's sure not at all my loss,
After all, I'm not the boss.

Yuh, I know it's a lousy point of view,
And a defeatist attitude, that's true.

Well, since I'm in the ring, I'll give my hat a toss,
After all, someday, there's a chance that I'll be boss.

And in the meantime, there's one thing on my side,
And that's to do my work with my very own pride!

LIFE'S WHAT-IFS

Oh, those twists and turns,
Those difficult ups and downs,
To our faces,
Bring on those frowns.
You can never know,
Those what-ifs around the corner,
And how uncertain life can be,
Ready to bring on a downer.
Oh my, oh my,
Life give us a break,
Hold off till tomorrow,
Today, save me that headache.
There will always be another chance,
To get it right,
If we only,
Get a good night's sleep tonight!

OUR FRIEND FRANK

We know him as a right jolly fellow,
He's caring and considerate,
Likes to talk, sometimes to be mellow.

He's a friend we can turn to,
A friend to have a beer with,
He'll be there whatever you have to do.

Give him a chance, he'll give an opinion for sure,
His life to all brings sunshine and joy,
It's said his life is like an open door.

Reaching out, his heart's in the right place,
Watch him gather strength,
With remarkable grace.

A family ever precious, so true,
That he knows how to treasure,
But what's in his mind we haven't a clue.

He teaches us a lesson good,
And we'd better off to listen,
He says, "Live a life of cheer," as we all know we should.

Happy Birthday

Birthdays may come and go,
But friendships only grow,
And cannot be forgotten,
Because our hearts you have begotten.

Bobby, you have done good for us,
Gave us the financial advice we trust,
Helped us with our electronic woes,
That Bob couldn't fix with what he knows.

So the years fly by,
And we can't say why,
That things can't stay the same,
And we really don't know whom to blame.

So we curse and shout,
Can't figure what it's all about,
Just age gracefully, they say,
Well, sorry that doesn't make my day.

We can only hope,
That we can cope,
When things get miserably wrong,
And gather up all our will and might,
Just enough to stay strong.

Happy birthday, Bobby. God bless.

A Poet's Thought

A poet's thought is as fleeting as,
A moor's fretful mourn on a faraway dock,
A smile in which to bask in,
A piercing seagull's cry,
The moan in a lover's tryst,
A light sprinkling of rain,
A secret's giggle,
A moment of truth,
The sudden prickling of terror,
And the whistle of a train just passing through,
It is as fleeting as a moment's chance to put it down on paper,
Then, forever it's gone, never to be recaptured again.

The Sheriff Always
Gets His Man

Watch out, all you bad guys,
Think you're tough,
Out there robbin' and killin',
And all that stuff.
For we got ourselves a sheriff mean,
And with him is the greatest team.
That's why the sheriff always gets his man,
He's got to be an ace as the public demands.
He's our leader, quite calm and cool,
Anybody that tangles with him is a gosh darn fool.
So there's one thing that should be quite clear,
If you value your life ever so dear.
Always obey THE GOLDEN RULE,
That you learned when you were in school.

IMPRISONMENT

Cold damp walls,
Gray everywhere,
Nothing much to do,
Except to ponder and stare.

Imprisoned behind these barren walls,
For wrongly deeds done to others,
Paying for my terrible guilts,
In this closed existence that smothers.

Too much time for regrets,
Many things left undone,
Times passes by,
I'm forgotten by some.

A time of trials,
Foolishness paid for,
Days running into each other,
Waiting, waiting for the open door.

Afraid to close my eyes,
Hate and violence prevail,
Rehabilitation is the only answer,
To change is what I must do without fail.

Else, I will perish,
Among here, the living dead,
Never to rise above the walls,
And these prison bars that I so dread.

I will heed society's call,
To stop the horror and crime,
And do my very utmost share,
By improving this one life of mine.

THE THIEF

Oh, hungry Squirrel, you,
Filling your tummy,
With the acorn's meat.

But along comes the Chipmunk,
And quick as a flash,
He can't be beat.

Steals your meal,
In the blink of an eye,
And leaving you feeling the heat.

Down his tiny hole he goes,
Leaving you mulling your loss,
Guess you've faced the bigger cheat.

DIVINE INTERVENTION

Sometimes when I take the wrong road,
There you go and pull me back,
I know I make mistakes,
But won't you give me some slack?
Life can be tough,
And downright confusing too,
Sometimes it's all uphill,
And you made us imperfect, isn't that true?

Friend or foes, who needs friends like that?
Give us a break, it'll take a while,
A century or two or three or such,
To muddle around is more our style,
We'll get there in time,
For you've promised that,
Have to get rid of all hate and war, poverty and disease,
You know you don't want us with you when we're still a brat.

We get many chances,
Who knows how many it will take,
You are patient beyond words,
This is very necessary, for goodness' sake,
Okay, here we go again,
Envy, a swear here and there
And as you pull me back to the starting line,
You're my savior,
And though it takes an eternity, you'll always care.

DREAMER

I am a dreamer,
Tho' the waves snuff out my flame,
Like the strong and forceful steamer,
My ambitions are hard to tame.

And so I will hold on fast,
Like the "Lady of the Torch,"
Gaining on speed at last,
No rocking chair for me on a porch.

Slowly, at first, then like a charger,
My spirit shall rise above,
Tho' doomed at one time, my faith is larger,
All I need is a little push or a shove.

Then I will linger on the ground no longer,
Head above the water as I breathe life back in,
At long last I am getting stronger,
Head up high onward and upward my chin.

The time is now ripe to move on ahead,
For I am a dreamer and master of my own,
My choice is made for a better life instead,
Defeated no more and never again shall I walk alone!

M. J.

Michael, Michael, Michael,
Gone too soon,
What happened to you,
Now, high up above, chasing the moon?

Is that where,
You learned "The Walk"?
And sure, we'll miss you,
Never had that chance to talk.

I would have told you,
What a gift you had,
To cherish it, protect it,
Don't let the roadblocks make you sad.

We enjoyed your short time on earth,
Couldn't get enough of you in the news,
But all those stories about you,
Jeepers, surely gave us the blues.

Whatever else, Michael, may your spirit now rest,
You gave us much entertainment pleasure,
So we'll take the bad with the good,
For to truly love is to love without measure.

Let's Go, Brandon

And,
Who the heck is Brandon?
Sounds like a good guy,
But boggles my mind,
And causes a great big sigh.

So,
Give me some leeway,
Or a clue,
If I don't find out,
I'm going to be quite blue.

Can't sleep at all at night,
Want to instead count sheep,
But there it goes haywire,
My deepest sleep.

When tomorrow comes,
I'll erase my doubt,
Find out for sure,
And then give a great big shout.

Let's go, Brandon!

HEAVENLY STORES

Are there any stores in Heaven?
How disappointed I would be,
To find out,
That they are not so necessary.

But how would I spend,
All the money that I saved,
For such a venture there,
And how good I'd behaved?

Where would the fun be?
No window shopping?
No sales to grab?
No credit card dropping?

I guess I'll just have to learn,
The more important things in life,
Family and love and hope,
And that there really is a place that doesn't have any worldly strife.

HOUSE OF THE LORD

Though my wants are many,
Here, on this earth of so plenty.
Though I feel so deprived,
I thank God I'm alive.
For I shall want no more in the House of the Lord,
There will be no need of earthly treasures to hoard.
Though I suffer pain and have nothing of value,
In the House of the Lord, I gain great stature.
For some, it's a dog-eat-dog and a money-conscious world,
To achieve only, or power obtain, so many are lured.
But if we stop and think and make some sense,
It's all in vain and such a pretense.
For in the House of the Lord, there are no needs,
Everything is there for everyone who heeds.

All About a Name

It's all in the name,
For better or worse,
And we've probably been told,
It can be a blessing or a curse.

A name,
Can cause some grief,
Possibly some harm,
And carrying it through life,
Might give one alarm.

So, parents, choose ever so wisely,
What you want the world,
To know exclusively,
That child's moniker you have ruled.

Choosing and picking,
From a list so gallant and galore,
For your children's future to bear,
Please know that it could be forevermore.

THE KENNEDY PARADOX

One thing is said but another often meant,
Politicians talk this but then do that,
So if ever rules were made to be bent,
A Kennedy is an expert and always up to bat.

For a Kennedy has mystique, they're so hard to figure out,
They are bold in character, with charisma to the end,
Special individuals, the world will long shout,
Having their share of sorrow and plight, all that life sends.

A mixture of mother and father, they're a paradox in flesh,
Who came together in marriage, however,
Did never completely mesh,
Though gave to their sons and daughters purpose forever.

Strength and weakness, a paradox they share,
They are "Heroes of Our Times" and this a quote,
They live, laugh, and play hard, beware,
And when in politics, they'll seduce your vote!

They try hard to make a better world for all to live,
And so aware are we of this "Camelot" they create,
We pardon their wrongs, as our hearts do forgive,
Oh, those Kennedys do take chances,
        and some on thin ice do skate.

They're daring and brave, all must acknowledge true,
Sticking together through thick and thin,
And their rewards are still long overdue,
So once again, pass the torch and let a new generation begin.

LIFE CAN BE FUNNY
(AND A BIT STRANGE TOO)

We don't understand,
Nor will we ever,
We just get up and go,
Push the button, pull the lever.

We can cry and moan,
Then laugh and dance,
Pick up the pieces,
Hold our very own, keep the stance.

Little by little, somehow get the job done,
Keep generations after generations going,
Raising families at our best,
And trying to "keep the ole' juices flowing."

It's a reality game of cat and mouse,
But fill each day with all that you can,
For we don't know when the game is finished,
And we are called back to where it all began.

Spiders

Yikes, my mortal enemy,
Do confound my senses,
Why am I so afraid?
Between us I need strong fences.

Stay away from me,
I plead,
Don't want you near,
Godspeed.

You have your life purpose,
And I have mine,
Nothing in common we two,
And never more us shall entwine.

Oh, when I spot one on me,
Hysteria takes over,
Panic, to say the least,
Run, I say and take cover.

I don't really understand,
This problem I have to deal with,
And though it soon passes,
It's just been with me since my birth.

What's that name they give it?
ARACHNOPHOBIA the experts say,
For someone else may have it too,
Makes me feel a little better today!

The Last Rose of Summer

Sadly gone, ever so soon,
Then along comes autumn,
A season changed,
But not forgotten.
The last rose of summer,
A fading fragrance,
And too soon the color,
And summer's last romance, per chance.
Oh, that perfect flower creation,
None other can match,
Every petal perfect,
Oh, you can reach out,
But not meant to snatch!

A Bee Sting

Oh, how it hurts!
Why did you do,
Such a thing to me!

Thought you were a friend,
Pollinating our beautiful blossoms,
Yet you turned on me, I see.

I stood there silently watching,
Mesmerized,
As you fluttered from flower to flower.

Carrying out God's plan,
Continuing His creativity,
With all your given power.

I'm sorry I stretched out,
Disturbing your action,
But caught myself too late.

Didn't know I was your intended next,
When I smelled that flower,
And that was my one big mistake.

THE NAME'S STILL THE SAME

As of this writing, I make no claim to fame,
It eludes me as the wild beast unwilling to be tamed,
It makes no difference, as I choose to keep my name the same,
There's no one to blame,
However, a bit of recognition would be such fun to this dame,
We all know that life's but a game of choices and some luck,
And I'll just say my "Thank you's" as I'm glad I came,
To this point in my life where tranquility will reign,
But sometimes, if I deign to complain about a little pain,
Let me say, you'd probably do the same,
Because we're all a little vain,
It's a tough battle for the meek and the faint of heart,
I know I'm as stubborn as a stain on a white cloth,
And I mean to cause no rain to fall, life's too short,
That's the main thing to know,
Just don't miss your train when the time is due,
There's just so much success you can obtain before,
The curtain closes on your mane,
Keep your chin up and head high, that's all one can hope to do,
And remain in this world of the mighty's terrain,
I just don't want to blame anyone, God knows I did my best,
To accomplish what I set out to do,
But I've run out of fuel and my life's on the wane,
As it winds up this show with retirement my next acclaim,
Unless you make it worth my while,
Pay no attention to my lame excuses,
And pull me out of the closet for something more appealing,
And for the record, to make sure I'm still sane,
Just say the word, and I'm back in the running,
The show must go and I'm a fool once again.

About the Author

Kathleen Dubé is a retired registered nurse residing in Massachusetts for many years. She has been married for sixty-one years and has four grown children, eight grandchildren, and three great-grandchildren. They are all very loving and special to her.